Y0-BEA-304

MONTANA

A modern-day cowboy, Virginia City.

M. Woodbridge Williams

MONTANA

Photography by **Rick Graetz**
and others

Introduction by
A. B. Guthrie, Jr.

COUNTRY BEAUTIFUL
Waukesha, Wisconsin

Arrowleaf balsamroot. One of the earliest blooming spring flowers,
it dots the mountainsides and carpets the prairies.

Backleaf: Hereford cows graze in the Flathead Valley. The Mission Mountains rise behind.

Garry L. Wunderwald

COUNTRY BEAUTIFUL: *Publisher and Editorial Director:* Michael P. Dineen; *Vice President, Editorial:* Robert L. Polley; *Vice President, Operations:* Donna Griesemer; *Vice President, Sales:* Wm. B. Chappie; *Managing Editor:* John M. Nuhn; *Art Director:* Buford Nixon; *Senior Editors:* James H. Robb, Kenneth L. Schmitz, Stewart L. Udall; *Associate Editors:* Kay Kundinger (House Editor), Wendy Weirauch; *Art Assistant:* Ann Baer; *Marketing Director:* Jeanie Holzwart; *Sales Manager:* Mary Moran; *Production:* John Dineen; *Assistant to Publisher:* Gay Ciesinski; *Administration:* Roy Adolph, Rita Brock, Karen Ladewig, Dolores Wangert.

Country Beautiful is a wholly owned subsidiary of Flick-Reedy Corporation: President: Frank Flick.

Copyright © MCMLXXVI by Country Beautiful Corporation. All rights reserved. This book, or parts thereof, must not be reproduced in any form without written permission from the publisher. Manufactured in the United States of America. Film processed by Crown Color, Fox Lake, Ill.

Library of Congress Cataloging in Publication Data
Main entry under title:

Montana.

   1. Montana—Description and travel—1951-
—Views. I. Graetz, Rick.
F732.M66   917.86′04′30222   75-34321
ISBN 0-87294-079-9

Sunrise on a marshy lake, between Browning and East Glacier.

Garry L. Wunderwald

INTRODUCTION

Montana is spectacle, contrast and contradiction. It is also big, the third biggest of the contiguous states, a fact that helps to account for its variety.

The westbound traveler, entering eastern Montana, will find his eye reaching, unimpeded, to the far kiss of earth and sky, reaching farther than he can comprehend, for the atmosphere allows penetration beyond belief. Proceeding, he will come unexpectedly on water courses, cut shallow or deep, and see, floating in distance, the punctuations of buttes. Still farther on, by squinting to north or south, he will make out the clouds that are mountains and at last see, ahead of him, what appears to be the terminal wall — the great, spiked barrier of the Continental Divide.

Abrupt on the east side, the wall allows entry through and over the spine of the continent to the gentler Pacific slope.

Wherever he travels, he will come upon grandeur, different in reach, height and coloration, but still grandeur if he has eyes to see. Not everybody has. A couple who had rolled across Montana's great plain once complained, "There's nothing there." Nothing. Nothing for those who could not feel the embrace of distance.

As geography brings its surprises, so does climate. Winter can be bitter, though not so bitter as strangers imagine. The dweller on the east slope, his body and house pinched by cold, looks to the west and southwest, knowing that the warm chinook wind will not fail him forever. Western Montana, stranger to the chinook, does not need it, for there the climate is milder, milder by and large than that far to the east. It is elevation and elevation alone that often makes Butte or West Yellowstone the coldest spot in the nation. Few Montana communities are perched so high.

5

The common but charming wild buttercups
bloom early in the spring.

Robert E. Miller

The variations of climate and altitude bring just as great variations of growth. Here are box elder and cottonwood and willow, there aspen, pine, spruce and fir. The spring flowers of the plains, the cactus flowers and wild flags, give way in the hills to balsamroot, gaillardia, wild roses, geraniums, lupine and — look low — to moss campion, forget-me-nots and phlox. The mountains offer asters, columbine, sego lilies, beargrass. The list everywhere is too long to recite.

Wildlife, east to west, changes, too — from sage hen and antelope and deer to grouse, elk and grizzly bear.

For more years than lie within the remembrance of the oldest old-timer Montana has attracted the brush and the camera. Charles Russell, the painter, and Laton Alton Huffman, the photographer, come first to mind, but there were others before them and thousands since then. Their numbers grow, for grandeur and color and contrast and creature are the stuff of art.

Only a brash man would contend that the paintings of later artists are superior to those of earlier ones, but who can doubt that photography shows improvement? It does so, not so much because of the greater skill of photographers these days as because cameras and processes have improved and the knowledge of them as well.

Here, then, are recent examples of that vigorous art as exercised in the prime hunting ground of Montana.

A. B. Guthrie, Jr.

Danny On

Bighorn sheep, Glacier National Park. The surefooted cliff dwellers have acute hearing and phenomenal eyesight.

Snow runoff from Mount Reynolds, Glacier National Park.

Backleaf: Lake McDonald, Glacier National Park.
A moment of overwhelming mood.

National Park Service, photo by M. Woodbridge Williams

An unnamed stream fed by melting snow flows over sedimentary rock shelves exposed in the Logan Pass area of Glacier National Park.

Lodgepole pine snow ghosts in the Rattlesnake Mountains
near Missoula. A combination of fog, frost, wind and heavy snow create
these winter sculptures common to the Montana mountains.

Mount Reynolds, Glacier National Park.
Glacier lilies, the first flowers of spring, fill the meadows below.
This area of Logan Pass is a popular tourist attraction.

Mount Clements, Glacier National Park. Glacier lilies signal spring in the high country. Deep snow on the north side of this peak makes it a haven for summer skiing well into July.

Warren Peak in the Anaconda-Pintlar Wilderness. Lupine adds shades of
purple to the greens of meadow grass and lodgepole pine of the lower slopes.

Black Bear Meadow in the Maloney Basin country of the Anaconda-Pintlar Wilderness.
A trout stream meanders through this haven for deer and moose.

Hikers and backpackers find
western Montana full of such delightful scenes.

West of Cascade, looking toward Fort Shaw Butte. Commonly seen in the Western states, a butte is a landform with steep sides that rises abruptly from the countryside. Highlands that used to surround it have been eroded away.

Sentinel Creek tumbles out of the Madison Range high country.

Early winter in the Hilgards. The back country
and the peaks will be once again sealed off — sometimes
for as long as eight months — during winter.

Square Butte, southwest of Great Falls.
Charles Russell often used this as background in his paintings.

Lake HaHand, in the Madison Range.

From the Little Rocky Mountains, looking towards Malta.

Madison Range of southwest Montana, big snow country.
Before the snow starts to melt, as much as fifty feet of snow will have fallen in the upper reaches
of this rugged country where some peaks go above eleven thousand feet.

From Sentinel Creek looking towards the Gallatin Valley
in the Madison high country. Boat Mountain rises in the distance.

The Beartooth Highway switchbacks near Yellowstone
National Park lead to an alpine pass at 10,940 feet.

Spring in the high country —
Twin Lakes on the Beartooth Highway
between Red Lodge and Cooke City.

Montana Travel Promotion; photo by Garry L. Wunderwald

Froze-to-Death Mountain in the Beartooths. Only moss and grasses live above the eleven-thousand-foot level, in the permafrost, tundralike terrain. Near here is Granite Mountain, highest peak in the state.

Gates of the Mountains, named by Lewis and Clark during their 1804-1806 expedition. Spectacular limestone escarpments rise many hundreds of feet above the Missouri River forming a natural gateway. This view is from above Mann Gulch.

Forests of aspen turn into seas
of quivering gold in fall. The fast-growing
aspens are usually the pioneer trees on burned-over
or cut-over forest lands, or on abandoned fields.

Spring in Big Hole country. A small stream snakes its way through meadow grasses.

Looking towards the Little Rocky Mountains,
across the fields of central Montana, near Zortman.

Snow-covered peaks provide a backdrop for the ponderosa pines.

From the top of Thompson Hill, south of Fort Shaw.

Hills near Helena verdant in late spring. Red Mountain in the distance still holds winter snow.

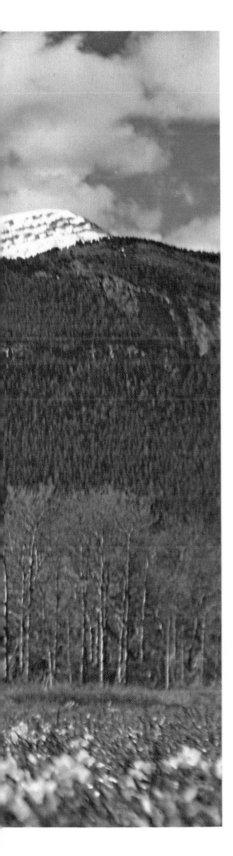

Storm over Castle Mountains, near White Sulphur Springs.

South Boulder River Valley in the Tobacco Root Mountains.
Two horses await their next trip up a mountain trail.

Garry L. Wunderwald

The stark badlands of Makoshika State Park in southeast Montana.

Glacier National Park. Hundreds of streams
like this one lace the mountainsides of Montana.

St. Mary Lake, Glacier National Park, is Montana's
most photographed lake. Beyond, high peaks are mantled by glaciers.

Seeley Lake in Swan Valley.
Ponderosa pines shade a spot that is very popular in summer.

Bighorn Lake, southwest of Billings, is a reservoir formed by Yellowtail Dam. The seventy-one-mile-long lake lies in a steep-walled canyon and is a recreational attraction.

Jerry Abbie

Rainy Lake, Swan Valley, in early fall. Very soon
the peaks of the Swan Range, in the distance, will be covered with snow.

Cox Lake in the hills above Helena. The lake mirrors
golden quaking aspen in the peaceful days of early fall.

Two Medicine Lake, Glacier National Park.
One of Glacier's most accessible lakes.

Fall on the east slope. Two Medicine Lake, Glacier National Park.

Lake Alva in Swan Valley. The dense forest of the Swan Valley slopes are home to the larch, a pine tree that loses its needles in fall.

Black Bear Meadow in the Anaconda-Pintlar Wilderness.

Overleaf: Earthquake Lake, Montana. A mountainside fell during the 1959 earthquake, closing off a stream which formed this lake.

Ed Cooper Photo

Dave Line

Lake of the Stars area of the Mission Mountains wilderness.
For the most part, the Missions' high country is void of trails.

Daytime rains in June often end with magnificent sunsets,
such as this one over Whitefish Lake in northwest Montana.

Don Wright

Don Wright

Missouri River—the "Big Muddy"—
rises in southwestern Montana and courses north,
then east, mostly through low-hilled prairies. Before railroads
crossed the land, the Missouri was the major
path that settlers took to the West.

Kintla Lake, Glacier National Park. Located near
the Canadian border, this is one of the best examples of pristine wilderness.

Marias River, south of Chester. The Marias flows through
northern Montana into the mighty Missouri River.

Missouri River, near Cascade. At this point, the river is clear and fishing is good.

Montana Chamber of Commerce; photo by Bill Browning

Powder River in southeast Montana
is a tributary of the Yellowstone River.

Blackfoot River, west of Lincoln. Cottonwoods, aspen
and brush ignite in a fire of colors after the first frost of the year.

National Park Service, photo by M. Woodbridge Williams

Glacier National Park. A mountain park has many moods.
The clearing after a storm is one of the most dramatic moments.

In early fall there are already ice chunks in small lakes
and the hills are patched with snow.

Big Hole River. Bitterroot Mountains
near the Idaho border are in the distance.

Montana Chamber of Commerce; photo by Bill Browning

Milk River. Fall in the prairie country.

Montana Travel Promotion; photo by Garry L. Wunderwald

John J. Craighead

Grizzlies, Yellowstone National Park. Catching sight of a troop of these bears is a rare occurrence.

Missouri River near Townsend. Hoar frost covers the vegetation.

Yellowtail Dam in the Bighorn Recreation
Area near Hardin, in the Bighorn Mountains.

Garry L. Wunderwald

Trumpeter swans, Yellowstone National Park.

Wild horses—offspring of steeds brought to the continent by sixteenth-century Spanish explorers—in the Pryor Mountains. Thirty thousand acres have been set aside here for the protection of these feral animals by the Federal Government and state agencies.

Michael S. Sample

The pronghorn, or American antelope, is often seen
in the fields and sagebrush country. Pronghorns are
small, averaging about a hundred pounds, and are said to be
the fastest running mammals on the continent.

Garry L. Wunderwald

Garry L. Wunderwald

Mule deer can be seen throughout Montana.

USDA Forest Service

A young fawn in spring, still showing the protective camouflage of a spotted coat.

Don Wright

Glacier National Park. The sighting of an adult moose
with its massive antlers is at once startling and impressive.

John B. Roberts

Gus Wolfe

American elk, or wapiti, near Gardiner.

Columbian ground squirrel, one of the smaller species of wildlife in Montana.

Ferruginous hawks live on the plains and subsist mainly on rodents.

Gus Wolfe

Swainson's hawk, a common hawk on the plains. Most of these birds winter in South America.

Thomas A. Moore

Montana Travel Promotion; photo by Garry L. Wunderwald

Sixty million bison once roamed the Western lands. By the 1880's, they had almost
been exterminated. Small herds are now maintained here and there, including the herd
of several hundred at the National Bison Range.

Garry L. Wunderwald

Monarch butterfly, Makoshika State Park.

Robert E. Miller

Carpet, or spreading, phlox is a low
plant which colors the hills in early spring.

Arrowleaf balsamroot has a strong and
overly sweet smell. There are about a dozen different
varieties of this sunflower-type of blossom.

Len Eckel

The purple of lupine and the scarlet of Indian paintbrush add splashes of color to a meadow.

Robert E. Miller

Ed Cooper Photo

Glacier lilies reaching out through snow are one of the first signs of spring.

Beargrass has small white flowers in a large dense cone. The stalk
is from two to three feet tall. At the base of the stalk is a large tussock of long
grasslike leaves which the Indians used to weave into baskets.

Indian paintbrush, a flower common to Montana
mountain country. The light purple blossoms are wild geraniums.

Robert E. Miller

Bitterroot, Montana's state flower. The fleshy root
was used by Indians and explorers as food.

Robert E. Miller

Wild geraniums, sometimes called
sticky geranium because of the coating of the leaves
or cranesbill because of its center spike. The geranium
is forage for elk, deer and bears.

Cedar roots, Glacier National Park. Like the hands
of old people, tree roots speak of the passing of many years.

Overleaf: Scarlet Indian paintbrush and white columbine
enhance the green summer carpet of a mountain meadow.

David Sumner

National Park Service; photo by M. Woodbridge Williams

Glacier National Park. Fires, some natural, some caused by man, alter the landscape each year.

Step Falls, flowing from Turquoise Lake to Lace Lake, in the Mission Mountains.

Helga Teiwes-French

Avalanche Lake, Glacier National Park. The lake is so named because avalanches often happen here in spring. Sperry Glacier is on the other side of the wall.

Glacier National Park. The forest rejuvenates itself amid the skeletons of burned trees.

Going-to-the-Sun Highway, Glacier National Park.

Garry L. Wunderwald

Overleaf: Sunlight playing through trees makes them look fragile and feathery.

Ed Cooper Photo

Montana Chamber of Commerce, photo by Bill Browning

Medicine Rocks State Park, near Ekalaka. The strangely eroded
sandstone rocks, around which Indians used to perform medicine dances,
look white under the noon sun and silver under the moon.

Garry L. Wunderwald

Makoshika State Park, near Glendive.
Erosion by wind and water has created these stark structures.

Sunset from Chinook,
near Lake Thibadeau National Wildlife Refuge.

Montana Travel Promotion; photo by Garry L. Wunderwald

The heart of the cattle and sheep country, near Big Timber, in south-central Montana.

Garry L. Wunderwald

Most ranchers corral the calves and use a branding table, but some cattlemen still use
the old-fashioned method of roping the calves out on the prairie and branding them there.

Garry L. Wunderwald

Grazing cattle near Helmville. Garnet Range is in the background.
Montana farms and ranches are large, averaging 2,500 acres.

Montana Travel Promotion; photo by Gary Breed

Raking hay by horsepower, Elk Park, north of Butte.

Branding calves near Boulder.
Each spring the new calf crop is branded and inoculated.

114

Garry L. Wunderwald

Garry L. Wunderwald

The annual buffalo roundup at the National Bison Range, north of Missoula.
Calves are weighed and branded and animals to be auctioned off are separated out.
Each year about seventy buffalo, or bison, as they are also called, are sold to control the size of the herd.

Garry L. Wunderwald

Modern self-propelled combines harvest winter wheat
from early August to October. Agriculture is Montana's number one industry.
The Highland Mountains line the horizon in this scene near Great Falls.

Garry L. Wunderwald

Grain elevators, northern Montana. Montana ranks
as one of the top five wheat-producing states in the country.

Summer's end, north of Helena. Hay is stacked in preparation for the long winter ahead. The hills beyond tell of a dry summer.

North of Choteau, along the east slope of the Rockies. Sanfoim, a legume crop, is in bloom
and winter wheat in its early stages. Clouds over the mountains will build up into a late afternoon thunderstorm.

State of Montana Capitol building, Helena.

Montana Chamber of Commerce; photo by Bill Browning

Little Brown Church, near Bigfork. This community church is interdenominational.

St. Mary's Mission, Stevensville.
Montana's first church was established here in 1841.

Montana Travel Promotion Photo

Montana Chamber of Commerce; photo by Bill Browning

St. Ignatius Mission Church, St. Ignatius, on the Flathead Indian Reservation. The murals (fifty-eight in all) were painted when the church was built in the 1890's by the mission cook, Brother Joseph Carignano, who had never painted before.

Montana Chamber of Commerce, photo by Bill Browning

St. Helena's Cathedral, Helena, patterned after the famous Cologne,
Germany, cathedral. Built (1908-1913) when Helena boasted of many millionaires,
the church is lavishly decorated. Windows were made in Munich.

Montana Chamber of Commerce; photo by Bill Browning

Soldiers Chapel in the Gallatin Canyon, between Bozeman and West Yellowstone.
Through the window behind the altar of this interdenominational chapel can be seen Lone Mountain.
The family of a World War II casualty built the chapel.

Robert L. Polley

Cemetery at site of Custer's Last Stand, on the Little Big Horn River.
Lieutenant Colonel Custer and his men were killed here by Sioux and Cheyenne warriors in June 1876.

Montana Travel Promotion; photo by Garry L. Wunderwald

Pompeys Pillar, east of Billings on the Yellowstone River.
Captain William Clark signed his name here in 1806 and his signature
is the last remaining evidence of his famed expedition. The pillar
is a landmark to innumerable travelers west.

Grace Lutheran Church, Barber.

Garry L. Wunderwald

Garry L. Wunderwald

Blackfeet Indian Reservation, near Browning.
A tipi is readied for an ancient sacred ceremony.

Garry L. Wunderwald

An abandoned barn near Augusta. The mountain range behind leads into the Bob Marshall Wilderness area.

Montana Travel Promotion; photo by Garry L. Wunderwald

Montana's first hotel is one of the buildings preserved at Bannack. Once a booming mining town in the mid-1860's, and the first territorial capital of Montana, Bannack is now a ghost town.

Montana Travel Promotion; photo by Garry L. Wunderwald

Ghost towns like Elkhorn, where once gold and silver mines produced $32 million, now stand deserted.

Garry L. Wunderwald

A memento of earlier days, Barber.

Frontier Town west of Helena, just below the Continental Divide on the east side of McDonald Pass.
A reminder of the formative years of Montana, it was built by John Quigley over the last thirty years.

Bald Butte on the Continental Divide, north of Helena.
The ghost town was once peopled by prospectors
who braved fierce winters in search of silver and gold.

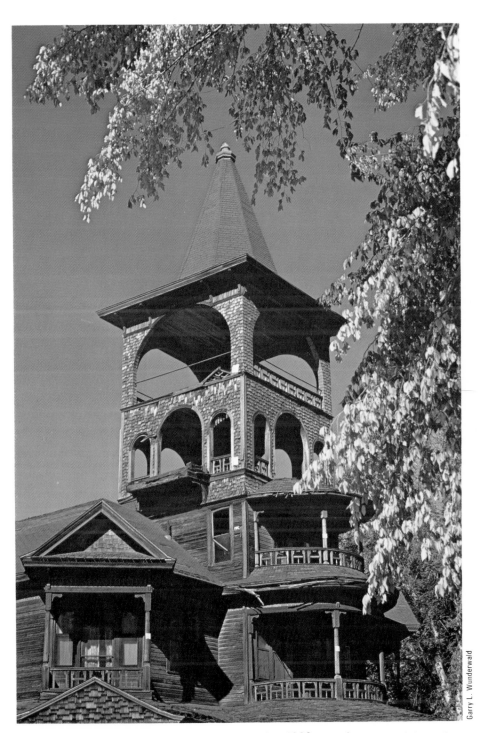

Garry L. Wunderwald

Broadwater Hotel, Helena, when completed in 1889, was the most aristocratic hotel of its day. Adjacent to the hotel was one of the world's largest natatoriums, which was severely damaged during a 1935 earthquake. The hotel, closed since the 1940's, has been partially auctioned off.

Ed Cooper Photo

A number of buildings from the nineteenth century can still be seen in Helena.

A deserted building near Marysville.

Montana Travel Promotion; photo by Garry L. Wunderwald

Buildings of eastern Montana homesteaders from the early 1900's have been relocated in a museum town called Daniels County Museum, near Scobey.

Montana Travel Promotion; photo by Garry L. Wunderwald

Virginia City, near Yellowstone National Park.
A century ago, during the affluence and ebullience of the Gold Rush days,
this town thrived as the second capital of the Montana Territory.

Ghost town of Garnet
is an eerie reminder of bygone days.

National Park Service; photo by M. Woodbridge Williams

Entrance to the visitors' center, Big Hole Battlefield National Monument.
In 1877, the Nez Percé Indians who had been fleeing to Canada were attacked
here by U.S. troops. The monument serves as a memorial to the U.S. soldiers
who died here, as well as to the fortitude of the Indians.

Garry L. Wunderwald

House in Martinsdale. Well-cared-for houses bespeak of the prosperity and pride of Montanans.

Mission Mountains Primitive Area in the Flathead
National Forest is a region of spectacular wilderness.

David Sumner

The sun backlights Rocky Mountain
pasque-flowers growing through fallen pine needles.

151

Bridger Bowl near Bozeman. Because of its unique location in the Bridger Mountains and its altitude, Bridger has the finest dry powder skiing in the West.

Skiers ply the slopes of almost thirty different Rocky Mountain ski areas in Montana.

Montana Travel Promotion; photo by Garry L. Wunderwald

Catching trout near Big Sky. Among
the trout varieties for which fishermen cast
are rainbow, Dolly Varden, brook and golden.

Montana Travel Promotion; photo by Garry L. Wunderwald

Rodeo of Champions, Red Lodge. The annual Fourth of July rodeo attracts the best riders from around the country to compete at such events as bull-dogging, steer-roping and bull-riding.

Montana Chamber of Commerce; photo by Bill Browning

Fishing for trout in the Smith River.

Montana Chamber of Commerce; photo by Bill Browning

Float trip on the Dearborn River.

Montana Chamber of Commerce; photo by Bill Browning

Float trip through the Beartrap Canyon, on the Madison River, one of
three streams which form the headwaters of the Missouri River.

Cox Lake, near Helena.

On Expedition Lake in the Madison Range. Often in late afternoon,
clouds in the west become part of spectacular sunsets.